A Note to Parents and Teachers

DK READERS is a compelling programme for beginning readers, designed in conjunction with leading literacy experts.

Beautiful illustrations and superb full-colour photographs combine with engaging, easy-to-read stories to offer a fresh approach to each subject in the series. Each DK READER is guaranteed to capture a child's interest while developing his or her reading skills, general knowledge and love of reading.

The five levels of DK READERS are aimed at different reading abilities, enabling you to choose the books that are exactly right for your child:

Pre-level 1 – Learning to read
Level 1 – Beginning to read
Level 2 – Beginning to read alone
Level 3 – Reading alone
Level 4 – Proficient readers

The "normal" age at which a child begins to read can be anywhere from three to eight years old, so these levels are only a general guideline.

No matter which level you select, you can be sure that you are helping your child learn to read, then read to learn!

DK | Penguin Random House

For Dorling Kindersley
Editor Kate Simkins
Senior Designer David McDonald
Slipcase Designer Stefan Georgiou
Designer Nick Avery
Pre-Production Producer Kavita Varma
Senior Producer Alex Bell
Managing Editor Sadie Smith
Managing Art Editor Ron Stobbart
Creative Manager Sarah Harland
Art Director Lisa Lanzarini
Publisher Julie Ferris
Publishing Director Simon Beecroft

Reading Consultant Cliff Moon, M.Ed.

For Lucasfilm
Art Editor Iain R. Morris
Senior Editor Jonathan W. Rinzler
Continuity Supervisor Leland Chee

This edition published in 2016
First published in Great Britain in 2005
by Dorling Kindersley Limited,
80 Strand, London, WC2R 0RL

Slipcase UI: 001-305129-Oct/16

Page design copyright © 2016 Dorling Kindersley Limited.
A Penguin Random House Company

© and TM 2016 LUCASFILM LTD.

A CIP catalogue record for this book
is available from the British Library

ISBN: 978-1-4053-0907-3

Printed in China.

www.starwars.com
www.dk.com

Contents

STAR PILOT

Written by Laura Buller

Into the stars

The *Star Wars* galaxy is a big place, with millions of planets in it – and it is yours to explore. But you are going to need a ride! Maybe you will take a spin in a speedy starfighter. Perhaps cruising in a silver starship is more your style. With luck, you will steer clear of the terrifying Super Star Destroyers!

In the huge *Star Wars* galaxy, you need space vehicles for getting around. There are thousands of different ships zooming among the stars. Some carry just one passenger, whilst others move an entire army. This book shows you all the important *Star Wars* spacecraft.

Welcome to the galaxy. Step in, buckle up and enjoy the ride!

Droid Control Ship

The Trade Federation is a powerful group of greedy merchants from all over the galaxy. Its leaders fly around in large, doughnut-shaped cargo ships.

The Trade Federation is unhappy with the Galactic Republic, which rules the galaxy. To prepare for war, the Trade Federation secretly changes its cargo ships into battleships. These can carry weapons and robot soldiers called battle droids.

Tough stuff
The Droid Control Ship carries over 500 armoured transports. These tough vehicles can break through thick walls.

The Droid Control Ship is the most important ship in the Trade Federation's fleet of battleships. It contains computers and special equipment that operate the battle droids by remote control. The droids will not work without signals from the Control Ship.

When a hailfire droid is after you, watch out! Each one is armed with 30 powerful weapons. These guns blast away, delivering deadly strikes as the droid races along on giant wheels.

The Trade Federation's leaders decide to show the Galactic Republic that they are powerful. So they attack the peaceful planet of Naboo.

Above Naboo, pilots control the Droid Control Ship from the ball-shaped Core Ship, which sits inside the outer ring. The Core Ship also contains the ship's reactor engine, but it is not well protected. A talented young pilot, Anakin Skywalker, discovers this for himself when he sets off a chain of explosions that destroys the entire Droid Control Ship. In Anakin's own words, "Oops!"

The Core Ship can separate from the main ship and fly about on its own.

Naboo Royal Starship

Inside and out, the Naboo Royal Starship is fit for a queen. Its engines and equipment are the very best. Inside, it is as beautiful and comfortable as any palace. Everything is neat and tidy, right down to the ship's wires and cables. The finishing touch is the ship's body. The starship is covered in shiny silver metal, a colour only the queen's transport is allowed.

Because the Royal Starship travels on missions of peace, it is not armed with weapons.

The ship's body has a shiny, mirrored finish. It is polished by hand.

Padmé's starship

After she is queen, Padmé Amidala sometimes pilots this slim Royal Yacht starship herself.

During her time as elected ruler of Naboo, Queen Amidala uses the Royal Starship to make official visits. Her bodyguards, loyal handmaidens and the ship's crew always go with her.

Podracers

Gentlemen… and scoundrels! Start your engines! Podracing is an *extremely* extreme sport popular in the *Star Wars* galaxy. Several dozen Podracers race at a time, ducking and diving through the course at speeds of more than 800 kilometres (500 miles) an hour. Pilots use every skill they have to avoid crashing.

Pilot Anakin Skywalker sits in the cockpit.

On the day of a big Podrace, you can almost taste the excitement in the air. Or is that the smell of the strong fuel that powers these super-fast vehicles?

A basic Podracer machine is made up of a cockpit, or Control Pod, where the pilot sits, attached by cables to a pair of engines. But no two Podracers are alike!

Two huge engines power the Podracer.

Podracer pilots add extra bits of machinery to their vehicles to make them faster and so shave seconds off their race times. Anakin Skywalker is the only human good enough to race. This nine-year-old boy is a skilled mechanic. He improves his Podracer, which he built himself, with spare parts he finds in the junk shop where he works.

Anakin's mechanical skills are matched by his amazing performances as a pilot. Podracing fans are still talking about his victory in the famous Boonta Eve Classic Race, in which he beat the race favourite, Sebulba.

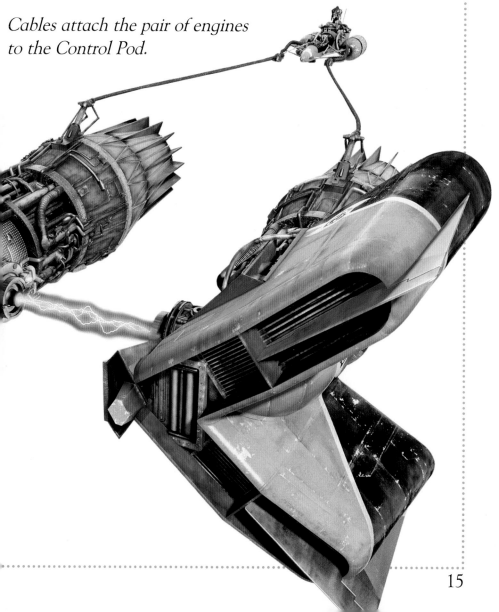

Sebulba's tricky tactics

Anakin's main rival is alien Sebulba. He will do anything to win, including throwing bits of machinery into the engines of other Podracers.

Cables attach the pair of engines to the Control Pod.

Naboo Royal N-1 starfighters

In times of peace, N-1 starfighter ships fly alongside the Queen of Naboo's Royal Starship. But if peace turns to war, they may have to use their twin blaster cannons to get out of danger!

One day, Anakin Skywalker hides in an N-1 starfighter. He accidentally turns the engines on, and the starfighter shoots into the air. It flies straight into a fierce battle between the Trade Federation and Naboo. Anakin dodges heavy fire from the enemy ships. He uses all the piloting skills he learnt as a Podracer on his own planet to enter the Droid Control Ship and destroy its engines. This ends the war because the Trade Federation's army is controlled by the ship. Anakin becomes a hero.

Slave I

When Jango Fett is after you in his starship *Slave I*, there's nowhere to run and hide. Jango is a bounty hunter. Often, he captures people who are on the run from the law and collects the reward for those he finds and delivers.

A good bounty hunter needs a ship that can reach anywhere in the galaxy. The ship must have a full load of powerful weapons to use on anything in its way. It should also have a secure place to hold captives once they have been caught.

Slave I is the perfect ship for bounty hunting. Jango stole it from a prison so it already had on-board prison cells, but he made lots of improvements.

Slave I *has special equipment that stops other ships from seeing it coming.*

Cockpit

Jango Fett's armoured suit and helmet hide his identity. He carries lots of weapons, including a rocket launcher.

The main changes Jango made were to the ship's weapons. It already had blaster cannons, but he added lots of extra hidden weaponry, including laser cannons and torpedoes. He also refitted the crew quarters inside the ship to make even the longest journeys possible. The prison cells were changed to coffin-like wall cabinets to make them impossible to break out of.

Jango Fett often travels with his son, Boba. Jango pilots the ship, while Boba watches and learns from his father.

All in the family
When Boba Fett takes up his father's job, he becomes the owner of *Slave I*. He adds even more powerful weapons.

Republic gunships

When the Republic's defenders, the Jedi Knights, are surrounded by Trade Federation forces on the planet of Geonosis, the Republic gunships come to the rescue. These ships are a key part of any successful attack by the Republic. They can move army troops right into position, then take off at speed.

Each Republic gunship can transport a team of 30 soldiers and 4 speeder bikes to hot spots on the battlefield. Its thick hull resists enemy fire. It can fly through heavy cannon fire and escape with only a few dents.

The Republic gunships can also swoop down to attack ground troops and land vehicles.

Gunners fire their weapons from gun balls. There is one on either side of the ship.

Jedi starfighters

In the heat of a star battle, every second counts. Jedi Knights like Anakin Skywalker and Obi-Wan Kenobi count on their starships to help them slip through a war zone unharmed. They often fly into battle alongside larger ships like the ARC-170.

Anakin is training to be a Jedi. His starfighter is small but powerful. It started life as a standard Jedi starship, but Anakin uses his skills as a mechanic to constantly improve the vessel. He removed heavy flight instruments and bulky shields for greater speed and control. He even changed its colour to yellow to remind him of his old Podracer.

Invisible Hand

The Trade Federation's flagship, *Invisible Hand*, is the most advanced starship in the fleet. Its shields and super-thick hull help to protect it from attack by enemy ships.

In one incredible battle, the leader of the Republic, Chancellor Palpatine, is captured and held prisoner on the ship.

The Republic's ARC-170 ships blast the Invisible Hand *with deadly laser fire.*

Obi-Wan Kenobi and Anakin rush to rescue the Chancellor. Inside the *Invisible Hand*, the Jedi defeat Palpatine's captors. But the ship catches fire. Even though it breaks in half, Anakin manages to land what's left of the vessel before it is destroyed by flames.

Escape pods

There are times when a quick getaway is best, especially when lives are in danger. For those times, an escape pod is a very welcome sight.

Most large starships, and even some planets, have escape pods. Smaller ships, such as starfighters, have ejector seats.

Droid friends R2-D2 and C-3PO get out of a tricky situation in this escape pod.

Yoda's lucky escape
Jedi master Yoda found himself
in a tight spot on the Wookiee
home planet of Kashyyyk.
So, he boarded this pod, pressed
the escape button and sailed away.

These special ejector seats throw the pilot
out of a damaged ship to safety.

Escape pods are like lifeboats.
Some are only big enough for one person.
Others are designed to hold many people.
Once launched, the pods automatically
find the nearest planet to land on.

A typical escape pod has enough
supplies to keep the occupants safe
and alive until they are rescued.
Communications equipment means that
the passengers can send out calls for
help. They just have to hope that their
messages are received by someone friendly!

Imperial shuttles

The peaceful Republic has been taken over by Palpatine. He is really an evil schemer, whose only goal is power. The Republic is now Palpatine's Empire, and he has made himself Emperor.

Palpatine uses an Imperial shuttle as his personal transport. The sight of the Emperor's ship arriving like a giant bird of prey strikes fear into all who hate the Empire.

The shuttle's side wings fold down when it is in flight. They fold up when the ship is landing.

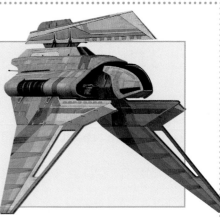

Palpatine's old ship
Even before Palpatine became
Emperor, he flew around in
his own personal shuttle.
This ship was smaller than
the later Imperial shuttle.

Important Imperial officers also
use these shuttles to get around.
One of the officers is Anakin
Skywalker, who has now become
the evil Darth Vader. Palpatine
persuaded the former Jedi
to join the vile Empire.
Each Imperial shuttle
can carry up to 20 troops,
as well as cargo. Blasting
cannons, shields and
thick hulls protect
the ships from
enemy attack.

TIE fighters

The small ships called TIE fighters are the main starfighters of the Imperial forces. The ships are simple and cheap to build because they are made in vast numbers. TIE stands for the Twin ion Engines that power these small ships.

TIE fighters attack one after another, sometimes hundreds at a time. A single TIE fighter may be easy to destroy, but for each one shot down, a thousand more appear.

Vader's own ship
Darth Vader pilots
a TIE Advanced x1 fighter.
It is faster and more
powerful than a TIE fighter
and has heavier armour.

To make these single-seater fighters
go faster, there is no heavy equipment
on the ships. The only weapons are two
laser cannons on the ball-shaped
cockpit. Often, dozens of TIE fighters
fire their cannons at the same time,
greatly increasing
their power.

Piloting a TIE fighter is a risky business. There is no life-support system on board so the pilots must wear a protective suit.

The ships are speedy and move around quickly, but they have no special shields to protect them from enemy fire. The fighters are easy targets from the side because of their large wings. It's a good thing there seems to be a steady supply of TIE pilots!

Bombs away!
Like TIE fighters, TIE bombers usually attack in groups. These bent-winged bombers are deadly. Almost every one of their ground strikes hits its target.

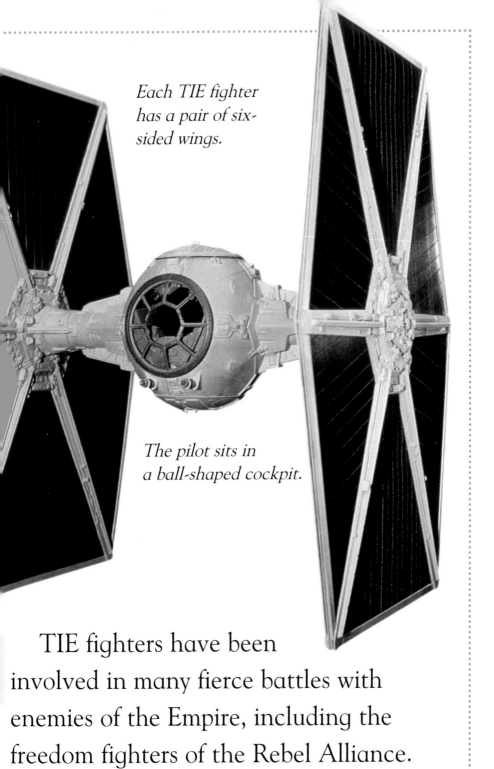

Each TIE fighter has a pair of six-sided wings.

The pilot sits in a ball-shaped cockpit.

TIE fighters have been involved in many fierce battles with enemies of the Empire, including the freedom fighters of the Rebel Alliance.

Millennium Falcon

You wouldn't know it from its battered outside, but the *Millennium Falcon* is one of the fastest vessels in the galaxy. It is owned by Han Solo, a one-time smuggler who fights with the Rebel Alliance against the Galactic Empire. The ship's co-pilot is the Wookiee Chewbacca.

The *Falcon* does not look like much on the surface. Its hull is beaten and battle-scarred, and the whole ship looks ready for the repair shop. But Han and Chewbacca have made many improvements to their starship over the years. It is even capable of outrunning an Imperial TIE fighter.

This is how the Millennium Falcon *gets its battle scars!*

Han and Chewbacca fly the Millennium Falcon *with C-3PO and Rebel leader, Princess Leia, on board.*

The *Millennium Falcon* is famous throughout the galaxy for breaking speed records. The saucer-shaped craft gets its super-speed from its hyperdrive engine, which Han has adjusted to make it go even faster.

The starship also carries a variety of powerful weapons, including laser cannons and missile launchers.

Secret cargo
Han built secret holds on his ship to hide smuggled goods. They come in useful when he and other Rebels have to hide there.

Han's starship has got him out of trouble time and time again. It may not be the best-looking vessel in the galaxy, but it never lets him down.

Han pays a visit to his starship's previous owner, Lando Calrissian. Han won the ship from Lando in a gambling game.

X-wing starfighters

An X-wing starfighter is the little ship that destroys the Empire's first Death Star, a huge super-weapon. Of course, Luke Skywalker, the brave young Rebel Alliance pilot at the controls that day, has Jedi powers to guide him. But his choice of starship definitely helps him to beat the odds.

Fastest starfighter
The Rebel Alliance pilots
also fly a ship called
an A-wing starfighter.
This ship is difficult to fly
because it goes so fast!

The X-wings get their name from
the shape of their wings. In battle, the
wings split into an X-shape. At the end
of each wing is a powerful laser cannon.

An X-wing starfighter fires on an enemy TIE fighter with its high-powered laser cannons.

The X-wings are the starfighters of the Rebel Alliance. These speedy starships are equipped with torpedo launchers and have special equipment to help guide the pilot.

The Rebel Alliance works out a plan to destroy the Death Star. If the super-weapon's engine can be hit by a torpedo, the deadly Death Star will explode.

To do this, a pilot must land a torpedo into a small hole in a deep, dark trench. The Rebel pilots are eager to have a go. Many try, but it is only future Jedi Luke Skywalker, with a little help from Han Solo in the *Millennium Falcon*, who hits the target.

After Luke blows the Death Star to bits, the X-wing starship becomes a legend among Rebel Alliance pilots. Could this be the best single-pilot starfighter ever built?

Something familiar?
Take a look at the split-wing design of the Republic's ARC-170 clonefighter ship. The X-wing starfighter is very similar to this earlier design.

Super Star Destroyer

Many things come in large sizes. Some things come in extra-large sizes. But the Super Star Destroyer *Executor* is so big, it is almost off the scale! It is the largest starship in the galaxy, at an incredible 19,000 metres (11.8 miles) long.

This terrifying dagger-shaped giant is evil Darth Vader's command ship. Its enormous size is a symbol of the strength and power of the Empire.

Frightening forerunner

Before the Super Star Destroyer, the wedge-shaped Star Destroyer was the Empire's most feared battleship. It was 1,600 metres (1 mile) long.

Darth Vader's starship is stocked with more than 1,000 deadly weapons, ready to use in any attack on the Rebel Alliance. It can also carry thousands of troops, starfighters, vehicles and other military equipment.

Darth Vader commands the Executor *from the bridge. The crew jump to attention when he speaks.*

The Super Star Destroyer's deflector-shield dome helps protect the ship from attack, and the communications tower makes sure the ship gets its messages across loud and clear.

The *Executor* is the first of many Super Star Destroyers to be built by the Empire to crush its enemies. But even these ships cannot stop the Rebel Alliance.

Republic assault ship
This massive transporter carries thousands of troops. The Star Destroyer and Super Star Destroyer are modelled on this earlier ship.

During one battle, an out-of-control Rebel Alliance A-wing starfighter crashes into the *Executor*'s bridge. The blast damages the Super Star Destroyer's controls. The giant ship can no longer resist the pull of the second Death Star, and the two collide in a spectacular explosion.

This pilot has lost control of his A-wing starfighter. It is spinning on a deadly collision course towards the Executor.

Glossary

Bridge
An area at the front of a large spaceship from which the ship is controlled.

Cargo
The load of goods carried by a ship.

Defender
Someone who tries to keep someone or something safe.

Droid
A kind of robot. C-3PO is a droid.

Elected
Voted for by the people.

Empire
A group of nations ruled over by one leader, who is called an emperor. Palpatine is the Emperor who rules the Galactic Empire.

Federation
A group of countries or organisations that join together because they have the same aims.

Freedom fighter
Someone who wants to be free from the rule of someone else. The Rebel Alliance are fighting for freedom from the rule of the Empire.

Galactic
Something from or to do with a galaxy.

Galaxy
A group of millions of stars and planets.

Hyperdrive
A *Star Wars* device that makes starships travel incredibly fast.

Imperial
Something from or belonging to an empire.

Jedi Knight
A *Star Wars* warrior with special powers who defends the good of the galaxy. Anakin Skywalker, Luke Skywalker and Obi-Wan Kenobi are Jedi Knights.

Mechanic
Someone who is good at fixing and making machines.

Merchant
Someone who buys and sells things.

Planet
A giant ball-shaped rock that goes around a star. Naboo is a planet.

Rebel Alliance
A group of people in *Star Wars* who have joined together to defeat the Empire.

Republic
A nation or group of nations ruled by a government that is voted for by the people.

Schemer
Someone who makes evil plans.

Secure
Impossible to break out of.

Smuggler
Someone who secretly brings goods in and out of a place to make money from selling them.

Trade
The buying and selling of goods.